D1211748

ENGINEERING
IN
ACTION

MECHANICAL ENGINEERING
AND Simple Machines

25 T

Crabtree Publishing Company
www.crabtreebooks.com

Robert Snedden

Crabtree Publishing Company

www.crabtreebooks.com

Author: Robert Snedden
Publishing plan research and development:
  Sean Charlebois, Reagan Miller
  Crabtree Publishing Company
Photo research: James Nixon
Editors: Paul Humphrey, Adrianna Morganelli,
  James Nixon
Proofreader: Kathy Middleton
Layout design: sprout.uk.com
Cover design and logo: Margaret Amy Salter
Illustration: Stefan Chabluk
**Production coordinator and prepress
  technician:** Margaret Amy Salter
Print coordinator: Katherine Berti

Produced for Crabtree Publishing Company
by Discovery Books

Photographs:
Alamy: pp. 5 bottom (Marc Hill), 13 bottom
  (Global Warming Images), 16 (Adrian Sherratt),
  28 (Nancee E. Lewis/San Diego Union-
  Tribune/Zuma Press).
Corbis: pp. 5 top (NASA/JPL-Caltech), 18 (Image
  Source), 20 (Bernd Weissbrod/DPA), 22 (Srdjan
  Suki/EPA), 23 (Car Culture), 26 (Gerry
  Penny/EPA), 27 (Sergei Bachlakov/Xinhua
  Press).
Dyson: pp. 17, 19.
Science Photo Library: p. 29.
Shutterstock: cover (all except middle and top
  left), pp. 4 (Dmitry Kalinovsky), 6 (Mikhail), 7
  (Barnaby Chambers), 9 top (Noerenberg), 10 top
  (Sergey Zvyagintsev), 10 bottom (ra3rn), 11 top
  (Denis Nata), 11 bottom (Yuri Arcurs), 12 (Ingvar
  Tjostheim), 13 top (Afitz), 14 (Ljupco
  Smokovski), 15 (Denis Tabler), 25 bottom (Juerg
  Schreiter).
Thinkstock: cover (middle and top left)
Wikimedia: p. 21 (Joe Bibby).

Library and Archives Canada Cataloguing in Publication

Snedden, Robert
    Mechanical Engineering and Simple Machines / Robert Snedden.

(Engineering in action)
Includes index.
Issued also in electronic formats.
ISBN 978-0-7787-7498-3 (bound).--ISBN 978-0-7787-7503-4 (pbk.)

    1. Mechanical engineering--Juvenile literature. 2. Machinery--
Juvenile literature. I. Title. II. Series: Engineering in action
(St. Catharines, Ont.)

TJ147.S64 2013   j621.8   C2012-907859-X

Library of Congress Cataloging-in-Publication Data

CIP available at Library of Congress

Crabtree Publishing Company
www.crabtreebooks.com   1-800-387-7650

Printed in Hong Kong/012013/BK20121102

Copyright © **2013 CRABTREE PUBLISHING COMPANY**. All rights reserved. No part of this publication may be reproduced, stored in a retrieval system or be transmitted in any form or by any means, electronic, mechanical, photocopying, recording, or otherwise, without the prior written permission of Crabtree Publishing Company.

Published in Canada
Crabtree Publishing
616 Welland Ave.
St. Catharines, ON
L2M 5V6

Published in the United States
Crabtree Publishing
PMB 59051
350 Fifth Avenue, 59th Floor
New York, New York 10118

Published in the United Kingdom
Crabtree Publishing
Maritime House
Basin Road North, Hove
BN41 1WR

Published in Australia
Crabtree Publishing
3 Charles Street
Coburg North
VIC, 3058

CONTENTS

MACHINE WORLD

It is hard to imagine going through a day without using a machine of some sort. Pick up a knife and fork to eat your food, and you are using simple machines. Go for a ride on your bike, and you are using a machine. Turn on the faucet to get some water, and you are using another machine. A train is a machine, a vacuum cleaner is a machine, and a soda fountain is a machine.

The mechanical engineer

All of the machines we use had to be thought of by someone. They had to be planned and designed and made to do what they were intended to do. The people who do this job are mechanical engineers. Without mechanical engineers our lives would be very different.

Mechanical engineers design, make, and maintain the machines we depend on.

Engineers and scientists: Engineers and scientists have a lot in common—but there are some differences between the two. Science isn't about developing new technology; it's about gaining new knowledge about why the universe works the way it does. An engineer can take this knowledge and use it to make something practical. The scientist can tell you why something happens, but the engineer can tell you what you can do with it.

Out of all the different kinds of engineer, it is the mechanical engineer who has the widest range of jobs to do and who needs the widest range of skills. A mechanical engineer might have to design anything from the brakes on your bike to a remotely controlled rock sampler on a **space probe** to Mars.

The mechanical engineer deals with anything that is made to move and the power needed to make it happen. This can include replacement parts for the human body, such as artificial limbs and joints. The knowledge and skill of the mechanical engineer helps to make sure that these parts will perform perfectly.

Mechanical engineers are shown here test-driving the Curiosity rover before it is sent into space to investigate the rocks, soil, and climate on Mars.

Engineering students have to learn many practical skills.

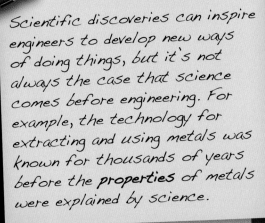

THE MYSTERY OF METALS

*Scientific discoveries can inspire engineers to develop new ways of doing things, but it's not always the case that science comes before engineering. For example, the technology for extracting and using metals was known for thousands of years before the **properties** of metals were explained by science.*

ENERGY, FORCE, AND MOTION

The mechanical engineer has to understand how and why things move. This involves dealing with some of the most fundamental things in the universe—force and energy.

What is a force?

In simple terms, forces are pushes and pulls. Forces are in action all of the time, on us and on everything around us. Forces are what make things move and change direction, speed up or slow down, or stop moving. If you push or pull something, if you stretch it, squeeze it, bend it, or twist it, you are exerting a force.

Friction

One of the most important forces at work in a machine with moving parts is friction. Friction is the force that causes objects to slow down and come to a stop. It occurs when moving parts rub against each other and acts against the direction of motion. The rougher the objects, the greater the friction will be. One way to reduce friction is by having highly polished surfaces.

The mechanical engineer has to take into account the different forces acting on a moving object, such as a car.

weight

reaction force

driving force

friction

air resistance

Forces and energy: Energy makes things happen. When a force acts on something, whether pushing it or pulling it, it means that energy is being transferred from one place to another. You can't apply a force unless you use energy. To get your bicycle wheels spinning, **chemical energy** stored in your leg muscles becomes **kinetic energy** (movement energy) pushing the pedals and turning the wheels.

Forces and motion: A mechanical engineer needs to know how much energy it takes to get something moving, to make it change direction, or to bring it to a stop. The mechanical engineer needs to calculate the forces that act on a moving piece of machinery, whether it is the spinning hard drive in a computer, an artificial heart, or an aircraft's tail rudder, and he or she has to design the machinery so it will cope with these forces.

Lubrication—using a thin layer of oil or grease—is a way of cutting down friction.

LOSING ENERGY

Friction converts kinetic energy into heat energy, which can't be used to do any useful work. It is one of the main ways in which energy is lost in machines, so it is a big concern for the mechanical engineer. About one-fifth of the energy used by a car is simply lost as friction between the moving parts.

WHAT IS A MACHINE?

What do we actually mean by a "machine?" A machine is a tool—it is something that makes it easier to do a task. It can be as simple as a lever or as complex as an **automated** car assembly line.

Simple machines

Simple machines direct a force from one place to another. A force is applied at one part of the machine. This force is called the effort. The effort moves another part of the machine that overcomes a resisting force, called the load. For example, if you push a shopping cart, you are applying an effort to move the wheels of the cart, which allows you to move a heavier load—the groceries—than you could manage if you tried to carry it yourself.

Egyptian engineers used inclined planes to raise the heavy blocks used for building the pyramids.

The inclined plane: A machine can be a very simple thing. The inclined plane is just a slope, or ramp. It is an example of a force magnifier. Using an inclined plane makes it much easier to raise an object to a higher level. Although the distance the object has to be moved along the ramp is much greater than the distance it moves upward, it takes less force to move it than would be needed if it was hoisted directly upward.

The wedge: A wedge is an inclined plane on the move. A wedge can push against an object with much greater force than it takes to set the wedge into motion. For example, the blade of an axe is a swiftly moving wedge that can be used to split logs. The sharper the wedge the greater the force produced. A wedge can be used to split objects or to hold something apart or back.

An axe delivers enough force to split a log.

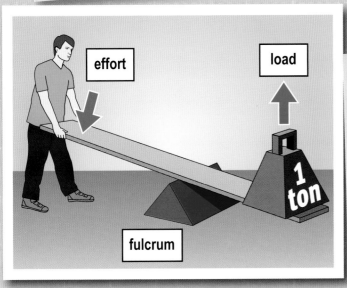

effort

load

1 ton

fulcrum

A lever can be used to lift heavy objects.

The lever: The lever is one of the most common simple machines. A lever is used to apply a force to an object that can turn freely around a fixed point, called a pivot or fulcrum. You can use a lever to lift things up or to turn things around.

THE EASY WAY TO CLOSE A DOOR

The farther away from the fulcrum the effort force is applied, the greater its effect will be. See this for yourself by trying to close a door by pushing it near the hinges (the fulcrum). It takes a bit of effort doesn't it? Now push at the edge of the door and you'll find that it's much easier!

LOOKING AT LEVERS

A lever is a force magnifier. Exerting a small force over a large distance at one end of the lever produces a large force over a small distance at the other end. It was this property of levers that led Archimedes, a scientist of ancient Greece, to say that if he had a lever that was long enough he could move the whole world.

Levers are used every day in many ways. Some of them you might not think of as levers at all. For instance, a pair of scissors, a wheelbarrow, and a fishing rod are all examples of levers. The three different classes of lever are shown on these pages.

A first-class lever:
A first-class lever has the pivot between the effort and the load. A crowbar is an example of this type of lever, and so is a spade that you use to dig the garden.

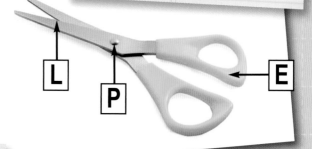

L P E

Scissors are a pair of first-class levers working together.

KEY:
E=Effort
P=Pivot
L=Load

A second-class lever:
A wheelbarrow is an example of a second-class lever. This has the load between the effort and the pivot. The load is whatever you are carrying in the barrow, the effort comes from pushing on the barrow, and the pivot is the barrow's wheel.

Moving patio blocks around with a wheelbarrow is much easier than carrying them yourself without using a lever.

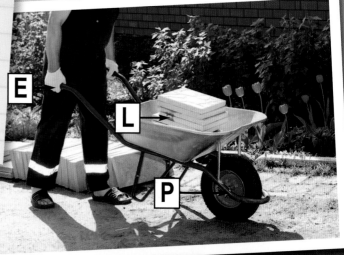

E L P

A third-class lever: In a third-class lever, the effort lies between the load and the pivot. It is different from the first two. Rather than being a force magnifier, it is a **distance magnifier**. The load moves farther than the effort, which is the opposite of the other two levers. A fishing rod is an example of a third-class lever. A fairly small flick of the wrist becomes a large movement at the end of the rod. In this case, your wrist is the pivot of the lever.

Just a flick of the wrist sends the fisherman's line a long way out over the river.

LEVERS IN THE HUMAN BODY

The muscles and bones in your body act like levers. For example, to pick up a weight (the load) you raise your forearm. Your bicep muscle provides the force by pulling on the bone in your forearm, and your elbow acts as the pivot. The muscle only has to contract a little to move the forearm a long way. Can you figure out what class of lever is pictured here? It is a third-class lever. Most of the levers in the body are third-class, which give speed and range of motion.

INVENTING THE WHEEL
(AND OTHER TURNING THINGS)

The wheel is one of the greatest inventions in history. The best guess is that it was invented about 5,000 years ago. It is hard to imagine how civilization could have developed without it. Look around you and try to imagine a world without wheels in it.

A wheel and **axle** work together as basically a rotating lever. A lever moves through an angle, but an axle and wheel make complete revolutions, or turns, through a circle. The axle acts like a third-class lever—a distance magnifier. If the wheel is turned, it acts like a force magnifier on the axle. This is how a car's steering wheel works, for example.

Cranes make moving heavy objects much easier.

Pulleys: A pulley is like a wheel and axle with a rope running along a groove around the rim of the wheel. Pulling down on one end of the rope moves a load on the other end upward. A simple single-wheeled pulley changes the direction of the force being applied. If more wheels are added, the same effort will lift a greater load. By using a system of pulleys, you could lift an object many times heavier than you could move without any pulleys. Cranes, for example, use a system of pulleys to lift large objects.

The screw

Screws are one of the most common attaching devices, used to hold all kinds of machine parts together. It is possible to think of a screw as a twisting inclined plane. Think of the thread, or spiral ridge, of the screw as being like a ramp going around the central shaft, or rod, of the screw. Turning the screw makes it move backward or forward along the thread as if going up and down the slope of the ramp. A screw with the threads close together turns with less effort, but you will need to turn it many times to tighten it.

A screw is an inclined plane wound around a central shaft.

These giant screws are used to raise water for generating electricity.

THE INGENIOUS ARCHIMEDES

In ancient times, the screw wasn't used to attach things together. A Greek inventor named Archimedes invented a screw that was used for raising water. It was enclosed inside a tube with one end in the water. When a handle at the other end was turned, the screw rotated and the water was drawn up along the thread of the screw. Archimedes is also credited with the invention of the compound pulley, a device he demonstrated by using it to haul a ship onto the shore single-handed.

COMPOUND MACHINES

All of the machines we've looked at on the previous four pages are classified as simple machines. Each one—the inclined plane, wedge, lever, screw, wheel and axle, and pulley—is used to change the **magnitude** or the direction of a force.

Putting it together

A simple machine might not be enough on its own to accomplish what you need to do. But if you put two or more simple machines together, you can make a compound machine. One of the simplest examples of a compound machine is the axe. An axe is a combination of a lever (the handle) and a wedge (the blade). The handle-lever acts as a force magnifier so that the blade-wedge strikes the wood with greater force.

Building a bicycle

A bicycle is a more complex compound machine than an axe. It has wheels and axles, levers (the brakes), and **nuts** and bolts to hold it all together. A bolt is another example of the inclined plane in action. It is very similar to a screw but is fastened in position by threading it into a nut.

brake lever

wheel

gears

axle

*The bicycle is one of the most **efficient** machines ever invented. A small effort can produce a big result.*

Getting in gear: Gears are an important part of the bicycle. A gear is a component well known to all mechanical engineers and found in many mechanical devices. There are different types of gears, but basically gears are wheels with teeth that interlock with each other in pairs, or that are joined together by a belt. Usually one gear wheel is larger than its partner.

Gears can be used to increase speed or force. When you pedal your bike, the effort you use is transferred along the chain and turns the rear-wheel **sprocket**. The sprocket then turns the bike's back wheel. A small sprocket will turn the wheel quickly allowing you to get up to high speed on a level surface or going downhill. Going uphill, a larger sprocket is better because it makes the rear wheel turn more slowly but with more force. Most bikes have a number of different-sized, rear-wheel sprockets that can be selected by a gear-changing mechanism.

The gear wheels inside this watch ensure that it keeps time accurately.

GEAR HUNT

How many machines can you think of that use gears? A car is an obvious example, but what about a lawnmower, a salad spinner, or an old clock that needs winding? See how many more you can find. Once you start looking, you are bound to start finding gears everywhere!

15

WHAT DO WE WANT TO MAKE?

People are always looking for new ways to do things, to make machines that are cheaper to run, more efficient, more reliable, faster, or more powerful than before. But if you want to know whether or not your idea will work, you'll have to ask a mechanical engineer.

If we want to make sure that the machine we are going to make will be successful there are a number of steps to go through. The first of these is to be clear about why we need the machine.

What's the problem? Mechanical engineers are involved at the very earliest stages of development of a new machine. The first thing to ask is what is the machine for? What is the problem we are going to use the machine to solve? Let's say we want a new vacuum cleaner that's really good at picking up pet hair. What do we need to do to solve that problem?

British inventor James Dyson, seen here at his drawing board, is famous for his engineering of vacuum cleaners that pivot on a ball.

Working together

Scientists and engineers work alongside each other to try to determine how best to deal with the problem they are trying to solve. For example, a scientist working with materials will know about the properties of different materials. A mechanical engineer will be able to figure out how these materials can be put together to make an efficient machine. Together they will gather as much information as they can that relates to the problem to be solved.

A handheld vacuum cleaner

Steps in the design process:

Identify the problem

↓

Identify criteria and constraints

↓

Brainstorm possible solutions

↓

Select a design

↓

Build a model or prototype

↻ (Refine the design ← Test the model and evaluate)

Refine the design   **Test the model and evaluate**

↓

Share the solution

Setting the conditions: There are usually conditions we have to meet in solving any problem. These conditions are often referred to as criteria—the standards we want to meet; and constraints—the limits or restrictions on what we can actually do.

For example, in the case of the pet hair vacuum cleaner, because it is intended for everyday use, it will have to be reasonably inexpensive to make. It should use power efficiently and have a mechanism that removes hair effectively. It should also be made using durable materials, but its design must appeal to buyers, too.

Setting conditions is a vital part of the process. It could be costly and time consuming to change things later.

17

SEARCHING FOR SOLUTIONS

Now we know what we want to do, and we also know the conditions we have to meet. The next step is to look for practical solutions to the problem we have set ourselves. Sometimes the answer might come to a single person in what is called a **eureka moment**, when he or she suddenly has a brilliant idea. More often though, a team of engineers will get together for a brainstorming session.

Brainstorming: In a brainstorming session people start throwing ideas at each other. Some of these ideas might be totally off the wall, but they could act as triggers for other ideas that work better. The key to good brainstorming is not to reject or criticize suggestions but to let the ideas flow. This is a good way of coming up with different solutions to the problem.

Engineers get together in a brainstorming session to share ideas and find answers to their design problems.

Ideas and possibilities

If all goes well, the brainstorming session should produce a number of ideas—some of which might raise other problems that the team will need to solve.

Will the vacuum cleaner be pulled along the floor or will it be handheld? If it moves on the floor, it will need some sort of wheels. If it is handheld, then weight becomes more of an issue—what are the lightest, strongest materials that would be suitable? To keep the weight down, the motor could be smaller and less powerful. Would a handheld vacuum be plugged into the household's power source while in use or would it have a rechargeable battery pack? A battery pack would add to the weight but the vacuum would be easier to use without a power cord trailing behind. Would a spinning brush get the hairs out of the carpet effectively? What could be done to prevent longer hairs tangling the brush and stopping it from spinning?

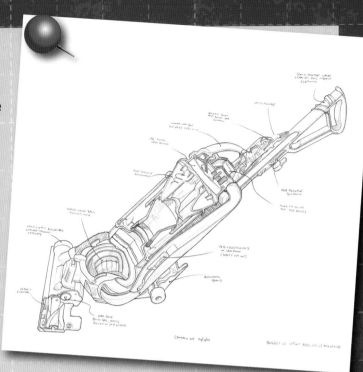

Sketches help engineers to figure out their ideas.

These problems all have to be considered by the engineering design team. The engineers will make sketch after sketch of their ideas, using computer graphics and good old-fashioned pencil and paper as they refine their designs, until finally the best design for the machine has been agreed on.

EARLY VACUUMS

Early solutions to the problem of how to get a vacuum cleaner to suck up dirt were not ones we'd find acceptable today. English engineer Walter Griffiths invented a device in 1905 that required the user to pump a **bellows** by hand as they moved it along. Another idea of the time was a gasoline-powered, horse-drawn cleaner that parked in the street and cleaned rooms by sticking hoses through the windows!

BUILDING A PROTOTYPE

Once an idea for an invention has been thought out and designed, the next step is to build it and find out if it actually works. This involves making a prototype.

First model: The word prototype actually means "first model." It is a first working model of the machine that can be tested in all possible ways to uncover any flaws in the design.

This is the engineer's chance to test how different components work together. Any problems that have been overlooked in the design should become more obvious when the prototype is tested. The prototype will be made using materials that are easy to work with and probably cheaper than those that will be used in the finished product. This allows changes to be made quickly and easily.

TESTING TIMES

Sometimes the prototype might be tested to the point of destruction. Testing a product under such severe conditions that it breaks down and fails can be of great value to the engineer. It helps determine safety limits for using the actual product.

An engineer tests how a new car stands up to extreme conditions in a **wind tunnel**.

Expected failure

No one really expects a prototype to work perfectly the first time. In August 2012, NASA engineers at the Kennedy Space Center were testing a prototype moon-lander called *Morpheus*. The spacecraft was equipped with rocket engines that were designed to lift it off the ground. Unfortunately, seconds after the engines were fired, *Morpheus* rolled over and crashed to the ground because one of its components had failed. Afterwards NASA said, "Failures such as these were anticipated prior to the test and are part of the development process for any complex spaceflight hardware."

BACK TO THE DRAWING BOARD

If something that looked good at the design stage fails to perform as expected when the prototype is made and tested, the engineers will go "back to the drawing board," which means they will try to come up with a better design.

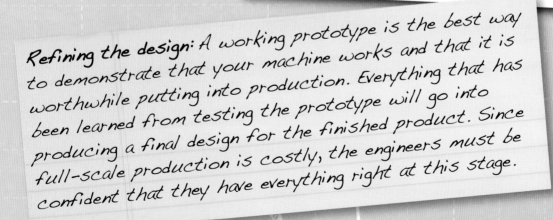

A prototype of the Morpheus moon-lander undergoes testing.

Refining the design: A working prototype is the best way to demonstrate that your machine works and that it is worthwhile putting into production. Everything that has been learned from testing the prototype will go into producing a final design for the finished product. Since full-scale production is costly, the engineers must be confident that they have everything right at this stage.

INTO PRODUCTION

Once the prototype has been tested and improved and the design has been finalized, the machine can go into production. Whether producing only one, such as a **satellite**, or something to be produced in large numbers, such as a car or a new vacuum cleaner, setting up the production process is another task that will require the skills of the mechanical engineer.

Production blueprints: The rough sketches that the engineers produced for their early designs are not much use at this stage. What is needed now is a highly detailed diagram showing all of the parts of the product and how they fit together. This is called a blueprint. If you have ever followed the instructions to make a model aircraft you will know how important it is to make sure that each part goes in the right place!

A team of mechanical engineers work to get a Formula 1 car in top racing condition.

On the production line

Many products are assembled on a production line. Originally production lines were entirely operated by people. Each person on the line would have a particular task to do in the assembly of the machine. The machine being built would pass down the line from one person to the next until the finished product was completely assembled at the end of the line. Today, production lines are often controlled by computer, with the assembly being carried out by **robots** or by a combination of machines and humans. The assembly line is a very quick and efficient way of producing goods in large quantities.

Robots are used to put truck bodies together on this automated assembly line.

TOOLS NEED ENGINEERING, TOO

It is important to remember that the robots working on an assembly line and the tools used to put the parts of the product together, are also machines that have been designed and built by mechanical engineers. For a complex machine, such as a robot space probe or a Formula 1 racing car, the tools needed for its assembly may have had to be specially made and to have gone through their own engineering design process.

DESIGN CHALLENGE: ROCKET RACER

As we saw earlier, mechanical engineers are concerned with things that move. The engineer knows that nothing is going to move unless a force acts on it. Can you design and make a model car with a built-in power source that will provide the force to make it move?

1: The problem: Making a model car that will move!

2: Criteria and constraints: You need a source of power to supply the force to move the car. The power source will need to be light and reusable. You need to make a car body that is lightweight and easy to move. You need wheels that run smoothly.

3: Brainstorm solutions: What could you use for the car body? Perhaps an empty plastic bottle would work. What about a simple piece of cardboard as a chassis? Could you make wheels and axles from wooden skewers and bottle tops? Can you think of a way to attach the wheels to the cardboard? Remember the wheels have to turn freely. What can you use for a power source? How about a balloon for rocket power? How can you attach the balloon securely to the car?

4: Decide on your design: Try to bring all your ideas together in a design. The possible solutions shown on the opposite page should inspire you to come up with your own ideas. As you sketch your design, identify all the materials you will need.

5: Build a prototype: Get all the materials for your racer together and start to assemble it. This is your chance to turn your sketches into a real object. As you build it, you might find that ideas that looked good on paper don't work so well when you try to put them together. This is all part of the process. Engineers will often make changes to a design on the spot.

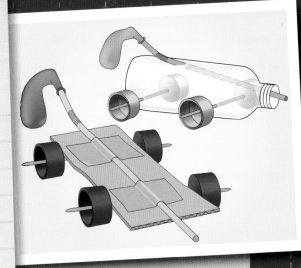

6: Test the prototype: When everything is ready, blow up the balloon and, fingers crossed, watch your car set off across the floor. Did it go as well as you expected?

7: Make improvements: Think of ways you might improve your racer. Could you add a second balloon for more power? Could you make the wheels run more smoothly with a little oil on the axles for lubrication?

Every moving object needs a power source, whether it is a balloon or the high-energy fuel mix used in a drag racer.

8: Communicate: The challenge of engineering is all about finding solutions to problems and one way to do this is by sharing ideas. Show your design to other people and ask them if they can think of ways to make it better.

ON THE ENGINEERING FRONTIER

What are some of the more challenging problems that mechanical engineers are currently trying to solve? Fields such as nanotechnology and biotechnology are at the forefront of engineering research.

Biotechnology

Biotechnology is mechanical engineering applied to living things. Bioengineers apply their knowledge and skills to solving problems in medicine and biology. Biotechnology has the potential to improve the lives of millions.

The study of movement in the human body is called biomechanics. Biomechanical engineers can be involved in designing and making replacement parts for people who have lost limbs or other body parts through illness or accident. A great example of the biomechanical engineer's skills can be seen in the **carbon-fiber** running blades used by top-class athletes such as South Africa's Oscar Pistorius.

The athletic ability of Oscar Pistorius and the skill of the biomechanical engineer combine to great effect.

Nanotechnology

Nanotechnology is an exciting field for the mechanical engineer. It involves building things on the incredibly small scale of the nanometer. To give you an idea of how small a nanometer is, a page of this book is about 100,000 nanometers thick. Working at this level involves moving individual **atoms** and **molecules** around.

Producing technology that works on this scale is one of the biggest challenges for engineers and scientists. One problem lies in how to produce a nanoscale production line so that nanomachines can be produced in large numbers and at low cost. One method being explored involves using highly focused beams of light to position atoms.

3-D printers like this could revolutionize the way mechanical engineers design new machines.

INSTANT PROTOTYPES

We saw earlier how important it is for mechanical engineers to produce working prototypes from their designs. In the near future, that could become a lot easier. Imagine having a printer that didn't just produce a flat image, but an actual three-dimensional object. These machines already exist. As 3-D printers get more sophisticated, it may soon be possible for engineers to "print out" prototypes, allowing them to test their designs quickly and easily.

SO YOU WANT TO BE A MECHANICAL ENGINEER?

Whatever may happen in the future, there will always be a need for mechanical engineers. So long as we live in a world where we need to move things and build things and produce machines that work, we will need mechanical engineers to show us how to do it.

If you decide to become a mechanical engineer you might find yourself working on anything from air conditioning to advanced **aeronautics**. The field is as large and varied as the huge range of machines with which we surround ourselves.

A DAY IN THE LIFE

Kat Louman-Gardiner is a biomedical engineer at Vancouver General Hospital. She says: "My days can be widely varied. Some days are spent in front of the computer, but... sometimes I'll be in the lab all day helping run the equipment for a research project, or assembling, or *calibrating* equipment. My favorite days are spent in the machine shop; if we need a *custom rig* for alignment or for a specific test, it is often my job to design and build it."

These engineering students are working together on a robotic device that can be sent into hazardous and dangerous areas to transmit data to emergency workers.

THE REAL MCCOY

Have you ever heard anyone say that something is "the real McCoy," meaning that it is "the real thing"? Have you ever wondered where the phrase came from? One suggestion is that it refers to Canadian engineer and inventor Elijah McCoy, who invented a system for lubricating the engines of trains. The story is that railway engineers wanted to make sure they were using McCoy's invention and not some inferior copy. So, they would ask if a train had been fitted with "the real McCoy."

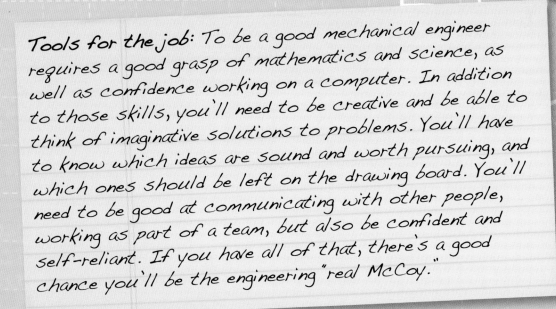

A sketch of the engineer and inventor Elijah McCoy (1844-1929)

Tools for the job: To be a good mechanical engineer requires a good grasp of mathematics and science, as well as confidence working on a computer. In addition to those skills, you'll need to be creative and be able to think of imaginative solutions to problems. You'll have to know which ideas are sound and worth pursuing, and which ones should be left on the drawing board. You'll need to be good at communicating with other people, working as part of a team, but also be confident and self-reliant. If you have all of that, there's a good chance you'll be the engineering "real McCoy."

LEARNING MORE

BOOKS

Nick Arnold, *How Machines Work*, Running Press, 2011

Tilda Monroe, *What Do You Know About Simple Machines?*, PowerKids Press, 2010

Chris Oxlade, *How Things Work*, Lorenz Books, 2002

Charles Piddock, *Future Tech*, National Geographic, 2009

Popular Science Magazine, *The Boy Mechanic*, Hearst Communications, 2006

Walter Ruffler, *Paper Models That Move*, Dover Publications Inc, 2011

Heather Schwartz, *Cool Engineering Activities for Girls*, Capstone Press, 2012

PLACES TO VISIT

The Works, Minneapolis, Minnesota:
www.theworks.org

Exploratorium, San Francisco, California:
www.exploratorium.edu

Welland Canals Centre, St. Catharines, Ontario:
www.trailcanada.com/ontario/
 st_catharines/visitor_attractions/
 welland_canals/

ONLINE

www.thinkmech.ca/kids/
Discover the world of mechanical engineering with games, printable pages, and links to other interesting sites.

http://discovere.ualberta.ca/Camps.aspx
Engineering camps for kids run by the University of Alberta.

www.discoverengineering.org
Lots of cool engineering stuff to explore.

www.geeringup.apsc.ubc.ca/
Engineering and science for kids at the University of British Columbia.

www.jamesdysonfoundation.com/
 scienceworld/
Visit this engineering lab to discover famous engineers from history and how things work.

http://pbskids.org/designsquad
Looking for engineering design ideas? You could find them here!

GLOSSARY

aeronautics The science that deals with aircraft design and flight

atoms The tiny particles of matter from which all materials are made

automated Set up to run automatically; once started, the process will run by itself without the need for an operator

axle A bar on which a wheel or pair of wheels revolve

bellows A device that produces a current of air when pressed

brainstorming Finding answers to problems by sharing ideas among a group

calibrating Checking the accuracy of a piece of equipment by measuring against a set scale

carbon fiber An extremely strong and light material containing several thousand fibers of carbon bonded together in crystals

chassis The basic frame of a car or other wheeled vehicle

chemical energy The energy in something that is released by a chemical reaction

custom rig A piece of equipment that has been specially built to do a particular job

distance magnifier Something that increases the distance over which a force is applied, for example turning an axle a small distance will make a wheel attached to it turn through a much larger distance

efficient Something that produces maximum results with the minimum wasted effort

eureka moment When you suddenly think of the answer to a problem. (*Eureka* is a Greek word meaning "I have found.")

force magnifier Machine, such as a lever, in which a small effort force is used to lift a large load

kinetic energy The energy that an object has when it is in motion

lubrication Applying something such as oil or grease to reduce the friction between two surfaces

magnitude The size of something

molecule A substance formed when two or more atoms join together

nut A piece of metal or other material with a threaded hole through it that acts as a fastener for a bolt

properties A property is a quality or characteristic of something. For example, one of the properties of metals is that they conduct electricity.

satellite An artificial object placed in orbit around Earth or another object in space; Satellites are used for communication and for gathering information.

space probe An unmanned craft sent out to explore space

sprocket A wheel with teeth on the rim that engage with a chain, such as the sprockets on a bicycle's gears

wind tunnel A tunnel where a stream of air is produced to test the effects of wind on models and full-size objects

INDEX